W9-CHK-643

MEDITATIONS

A Collection for Women

RUNNING PRESS

PHILADELPHIA · LONDON

A Running Press Miniature Edition™
Copyright © 1996 by Running Press.
Illustrations copyright © 1996 Andrew Powell.
Printed in China.

Library of Congress Cataloging-in-Publication Number
95-70145

ISBN 1-56138-688-X

This book may be ordered by mail from the publisher. Please add
$1.00 for postage and handling. *But try your bookstore first!*

Running Press Book Publishers
125 South Twenty-second Street
Philadelphia, Pennsylvania 19103-4399

CONTENTS

INTRODUCTION

*...often our bad moments are
self-propelled.... And the drama is almost
exclusively within our heads and hearts.*

—*Kathleen Tynan*
20th-century Canadian writer

Truer words have never been
spoken! How many times have
we worked ourselves into a near panic
simply by letting our thoughts run

away from us? And how many times have we been calmed and comforted by a caring friend or lover, whose gentle words of wisdom have steered us back to center?

Our thoughts are powerful indeed, as is the ability of the right words to influence where those thoughts will take us. *Meditations* offers wise reflections on subjects that women think about

the most, from love and friendship
to sexual politics and ambition. May
the insights offered here gladden and
reassure you—and spark new dialogues
of the heart.

FRIENDSHIP

Sometimes, with luck, we find the kind of true friend, male or female, that appears only two or three times in a lucky lifetime, one that will winter us and summer us, grieve, rejoice, and travel with us.

—Barbara Holland (b. 1925)
American poet

There are the families that we are born into, and then there are families that we choose— our circle of friends. While their faces may change over the course of our lives, the joy that they bring us remains constant.

Yet out of the many, we sometimes are blessed when one or two emerge as our steady, lifelong companions.

These are the treasured few who see us through a lens that is at once honest and loving. Like exacting coaches, they push us to be our best, mirroring the greatness within us when we ourselves can't see it, dismissing our self-doubts with a comforting wave of a hand, and bravely offering criticism when they know it's the last thing that we want to hear. They feel our

sorrows as if they were their own,
lightening our burdens by doing so.
And our victories? Their jubilation
doubles ours.

Like a seesaw, the friendship requires
balance. We respond to *their* ups and
downs just as they do to ours, offering
stability and security. Our phone call
to find out how their tough day
turned out, the card we send because

it reminded us of them—our friends
let us know that these things matter in
their lives. And, in our own acts of
giving, we find new qualities
in ourselves. We see that we also are
capable of making such differences in
our *own* worlds. As with the seesaw,
the friendship takes two, and the
discoveries that come from it cannot
be found alone.

True friendship requires true acceptance—and that means knowing when a relationship needs special attention, whether it means more time together or apart. No two people grow or change at the same rate, and there are times in the best friendships when breathing room is necessary. Sometimes the break results in a parting of ways, but other times the distance helps us to see things more clearly. Like fields left fallow, the friendship will be richer for the next planting, yielding a harvest more bountiful for the respite.

Whether short or long, past or present, every friendship is unique and brings something new and wonderful into our lives.

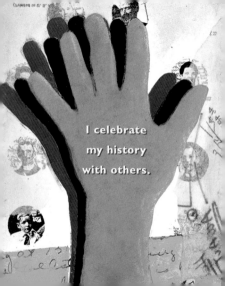

I celebrate
my history
with others.

SOLITUDE

Certain springs are tapped only when we are alone....women need solitude in order to find again the true essence of themselves; that firm strand which will be the indispensable center of a whole web of human relationships.

—Anne Morrow Lindbergh (b. 1906)
American writer

Solitude

It happens so often it's almost funny: We yearn for a moment's peace and quiet, only to turn on the radio, make a phone call, or run an errand as soon as an opportunity for solitude presents itself. "Life's demands are relentless," we tell ourselves. "I need to use my spare time to catch up." Is that really the reason, though, that we tend toward constant motion? Or is there something about the state of solitude that doesn't feel quite right?

After all, when it comes to relating to others, women are "naturals." With an almost eerie prescience, we are often able to sense others' thoughts and feelings before the words are actually spoken. This sixth sense, humorously referred to as "a woman's intuition," is as reliable as it is intangible, and renders a fullness and intimacy to our relationships that are deeply satisfying.

But if we are to stay in tune with our hearts—with the inner voice that affirms who we are at our truest—we need to connect just as intimately with ourselves as we do with others. In fact, the way in which we relate to others is often determined by how we feel about ourselves. Without this understanding, we risk damaging the very relationships that strengthen and support us.

Not so long ago, before life was invaded by modern luxuries like fax machines, beepers, microwave ovens, and even washers and dryers, the daily routines of women had a degree of

built-in solitude. Hanging a basket
of laundry or ironing linens slowed
life's pace to a rhythm that allowed
for interludes of daily contemplation.
Today's "conveniences," ironically,
have made such moments of solitude
hard to come by. While we can't trade
places with our female ancestors, we
can incorporate their value of solitude
into our own lives.

When we give ourselves the replen-
ishing gift of aloneness, we affirm that
we are worthy of the same kind of
loving and attentive listening that we
so freely give to others.

Alone, I am
in the best
of company.

IMAGINATION

...the key to life is imagination.
If you don't have that, no matter
what you have, it's meaningless.
If you do have imagination...you
can make a feast of straw.

—*Jane Stanton Hitchcock*
20th-century American writer

Imagination

The imagination is life's ultimate transport vehicle. Without requiring us to move a muscle, it whisks us into worlds purely of our own design. It lets us soar with eagles over craggy mountains, take an encore at the Met, meet the handsome stranger whom we see every day on the bus. Without consequence or disturbance, our imagination allows us to engage in rich fantasies where we can dwell for a few moments, free from the laws of nature or man.

But are we really only "day-dreaming"? When we were children, our imagination roamed freely for long periods of time, conjuring up fairy-tale kingdoms and imaginary friends so clearly that the line separating reality from fantasy often blurred beyond distinction. Because we were unimpeded by adult concerns, it was *never* time to "get back to work," so our imaginings ran their full course. But more than child's play was occurring: Our imagination let us be independent. We may have been too young to have a say about the practical matters of our lives—like bedtimes, mealtimes, and school—but we had the power to create our own world where *we* were in charge. And what better experience for the day when we *had* to take our lives into our own hands and shape it to our dreams?

Our imagination never stops sending us powerful messages about ourselves and how we'd like the world to change. As we get older, we begin to see how our dreams tie into our reality. It takes a delicate—sometimes difficult—balance to relate our daily routines to our fantasies, but how else can we visualize distant goals and start realizing them today? Our imagination gives us the confidence to chase our dreams when reality seems to resist our efforts.

Close your eyes, breathe deeply, and imagine who you'd be if you were free of society's expectations and your own

inhibitions. What would your world—
your health, your job, your relationships, your attitudes—look like? Where
would it take you? If you can imagine
it, you can empower it.

I create my life.

ike's shadow peopl
ways it's works agains
vanted to get involved
tered me the part in
static. You know, all a
al inspiration and we
lationship. The only t

Most recently, Jane wrote, along with her broth
Cirque, the screenplay that would blossom in
a glorious tale of a black family making th

AMBITION

I've always tried to go a step past

wherever people expected me to end up.

—*Beverly Sills (b. 1929)*
American opera singer and director

Finally, ambitious women are having it all.

After years of being exclusively mothers or career women, we've replaced the restrictive "either/or" syndrome with a resounding "*and*." It's no longer considered unfeminine to be ambitious, to use our power to achieve our goals. Women now occupy seats on the Supreme Court, in Congress, and on the boards of Fortune 500 companies—and they're not forgoing marriage or parenthood to do it, either. The lives of our mothers and grandmothers were limited by social convention; ours are limited only by the hours in the day and our own expectations.

The only struggle, it seems, is dealing with feelings of being overwhelmed.

Ambition

Forget the old days when we could choose only one item from life's menu; we now have the freedom to select as many as we wish. The new paradigm encourages us to know ourselves well enough to decide which choices are worth our time and attention. We can select with peace of mind, knowing that having it all doesn't necessarily require us to have it all at once.

But sometimes ambition is too exhilarating to let us be so patient. It's an energizing, inspirational, as well as challenging, emotion. We attempt to reconcile our natural tendencies to be team players and consensus builders with our desire to push the envelope of our own potential. But our personal goals and our empathy for others don't have to be mutually exclusive;

in fact, women are keenly adept at balancing the two. Our ability to see those around us not as stepping stones but as much-respected resources and vital supports ensures that we'll never be hurtful as we grow to our full potential. In fact, as we rise our strength and resolve will allow others to aspire, as well. By graciously acknowledging the contributions of others with each step

we take forward, we show the world
that our triumphs are too bright to be
diminished, too sweet not to be shared.

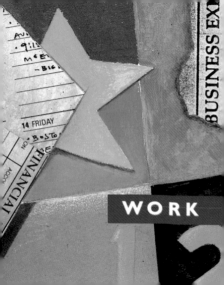

The days you work are the best days.

—*Georgia O'Keeffe (1887–1986)*
American painter

Work

If the benefits of work could be packaged in a medicine bottle and prescribed, what a potent tonic it would be! Self-esteem, a spring in our step, a sense of purpose, interaction with others, a stretching of talent—there is nothing like hard work to bring honor and meaning to our life and our world. We may fantasize about winning the lottery and never

having to lift a finger again—whether
to push a vacuum or punch a clock—
but chances are we'd soon feel the
need to exert and test ourselves, for
these are the efforts that let us grow.

Through work, we reaffirm to ourselves that we are independent people,
fully capable of taking care of ourselves
and earning our way in the world.
Whether we choose to do that by being

employed by others, by owning our
own business, or by running a household, the effect is the same. We've
made our mark on the world—we've
said, "I am here."

The challenge is to find the meaning
in our work; the good news is that all
work is meaningful when done with a
full heart, a sense of ownership, and
the greatest efforts that our talents will

allow. When we do so, we discover work to be an amazing teacher, revealing to us our strengths and weaknesses, talents and shortcomings, passions and dislikes. With this knowledge, we can make choices about how best to share with the world the gifts we are given.

So why do so many of us resist the call of the alarm clock come Monday morning? Perhaps because, more than

anything else, work is real; at the end
of the day, we either have something
to show for our efforts, or we don't.
This echoes the more subliminal
knowledge that, come the end of our
lives, we will either look back with
pride or with longing on all that we
have done. Work reminds us, continu-
ally, that we have a choice about what
the outcome will be. It calls upon us

to get away from fantasy and wishful thinking and into action. Through discipline and productivity, work provides the invaluable structure with which we fashion and attain our goals. It may sound cliché, but there really is no substitute for good old-fashioned work, nor for the satisfaction that comes from a job well done.

I can do it.

POSITIVE

THINKING

My deepest impulses are optimistic,

an attitude that seems to me as

spiritually necessary and proper as

it is intellectually suspect.

—Ellen Willis (*b.* 1941)
American journalist

What is it that allows us to hope? What spark of knowing resides in us that lets us look at even the most dire of situations and say, "Yes, but..."? To see the glass not as half-empty but as half-full?

Women who are positive thinkers are often cynically dismissed as Pollyannas, as though the practice of living in a state of hope is somehow simple-minded or unrealistic. The truth, however, is that those precious souls, who stubbornly search for the silver lining in the thickest cloud cover, are those who simply prefer to gain as much from life through joy rather than through suffering.

Still, even the most optimistic among us slips into negative thinking from time to time. If we're pessimistic about a situation, we needn't feel disappointed if things don't turn out the way we would've preferred. Nor do we risk feeling foolish if our expectations are dashed, or take the chance of feeling vulnerable if we've exposed our most tender dreams to the world's scrutiny. We are safe—or so we think.

Protecting ourselves in this way comes at great cost to our self-esteem, since we send ourselves the message that we are incapable of handling our difficult feelings, when in truth we possess abundant capacity to process, withstand, and overcome them with dignity, grace, and even humor. We may risk disappointment by setting our sights high, but the greater risk is compromising our abilities.

Cultivating an optimistic world view not only dignifies and celebrates life's wonderful moments, no matter how mundane or profound, but also allows us to weather life's sorrowful interludes with a particular measure of comfort. Through the practice of positive thinking, we are shown that even amidst the bleakest of winters, Spring quietly and patiently prepares her return.

When we practice the act of positive thinking, a two-fold miracle occurs: We reaffirm that we are women worthy of happiness, contentment, and joy, as well as replenish our reserves of strength and resiliency. Once more we have the courage to embrace life at its fullest—with all of its sorrows and all of its blessings.

I will take advantage of the good
and be patient with the bad.
Things always get better.

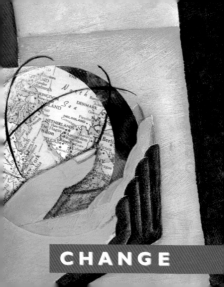

CHANGE

The one thing I've learned in this business—and in this life—is: whenever you say nothing is going to happen— something happens.

—Margaret Whiting (b. 1923)
American singer

Change

We know when we're ready for a change; we can feel it in our marrow. Despite our best efforts, a job sometimes becomes untenable, a relationship frustrating, the place we call home predictable and stale. The immediate solutions seem obvious: Quit the job, end the relationship, move to a new city. But while tempting, such instant gratification usually doesn't ensure long-term satisfaction.

One of the advantages of our admittedly too transient society is that we don't feel bound by duty or tradition to remain in situations that make us uncomfortable. Instead of really looking at the situation to see why we're unhappy, we institute changes that energize our lives. We deserve

such satisfaction, we tell ourselves.
Life is too short for anything less.

But are radical changes always the
answer? How many times have we
traded old jobs, relationships, and
cities for fresh ones—only to find
ourselves confronting problems similar
to those we thought we'd left behind?
It's possible that we're changing the
externals of our lives just to reassure

ourselves that we do have such power, while the underlying problems merely hibernate. Instead of simply reacting, we should direct our energies towards the more daunting challenge of changing from within.

Nothing is harder than amending old behaviors. Even at their most destructive, they are at least familiar and feel "right"; letting go of them

Change

takes away that dependence and makes
us feel like we're in free fall. We're not.
We are simply viewing the world in a
way that is more in line with our
dreams. When we forge internal
changes and become secure with
ourselves and our desires, we can
pursue with joy the external changes—
the new job, the new city—knowing
our actions have been prompted by

a sense of possibility, not fear.

When we're in the habit of fine-tuning our internal landscape, we find that we react differently to those changes that we cannot control. While we may not have a say as to when or how life's adversities will present themselves, we can always determine how we will hold them.

There are two kinds of changes—

those I seek, and those that

find me. I meet each with

confidence and strength.

SEXUAL

POLITICS

...what women want is what men want.

They want respect.

—*Marilyn Vos Savant (b. 1947)*
American writer

I t's hard to believe that sexual politics once prevented women from enjoying the rights that men have always taken for granted. The rights to vote, to hold public office, to receive equal pay for equal work, to preach from a pulpit, to establish financial credit, even to smoke a cigarette, to name a few, were never extended to women until the last century. As our laws and public institutions move toward establishing equality between the sexes, we owe it to ourselves not to take the legacy of justice for granted by tolerating the gender disrespect that sometimes occurs on a more subtle level in our own perceptions.

It's not an easy challenge. After all, most of us were raised by parents

whose gender attitudes were forged
during more conservative times; is it
any wonder that part of our emotional
struggle as adults is to shake off such
outdated notions? Try as we might,
certain qualities seen as positive in one
gender remain suspect in the other.
Men who go for what they want are
referred to as assertive, while women
who do the same thing are considered

pushy. The nurturing qualities so admired in a woman are derided as wimpiness in a male. Such stereotypes persist for a simple reason: They provide a framework—albeit an outdated one—in which we define our actions and observations. They allow us to remain in the familiar, safe from the pain and uncertainty of personal growth.

Think about it. The traditionally

dominant man need never examine his life; by always having the upper hand, he is always right. The traditionally subservient female need never test her wings and feel the exhilaration of soaring to new heights; by always serving others, she is always compromised. It is a symbiotic—though stagnant—system.

Yet, as the last century has shown, such systems and stereotypes must be

questioned and can be dismantled.
And what better time than now, as
the new millennium calls upon women
and men to cooperate on a different
level—to march shoulder to shoulder
towards a future that will vibrate with
all of the energy, talent, and strength
we possess, equal in dignity, beauty,
and respect?

I am an equal among equals.

SUCCESS

None of us suddenly becomes something overnight. The preparations have been in the making for a lifetime.

—Gail Godwin (b. 1937)
American writer

I t's hard to imagine a concept more loaded than that of success. When we're not yearning and planning for it, we're fearing or disdaining it. That's because common notions of success have to do not only with how things turn out, but with opinions—our own and others'— about whether the outcome was even worth the attempt. With that kind of

pressure riding on our efforts, is it any
wonder we feel conflicted?

The most nurturing mother knows
that the best way to build a child's
sense of worth is to encourage and
value *all* effort, no matter what the
result. So must we reassure the child
that resides within *us* that success is
about seeing life as an endless adventure,
with victories and mishaps as part of

the journey. Success lies in how we deal with each detour and obstacle. Viewed this way, life yields important lessons in all our endeavors, even those we deem failures.

History is resplendent with women whose lives show time and again that the coupling of vision with determination is the prescription for success. Suffragette Susan B. Anthony suffered many a setback in her work to secure the vote for women, but saw in each "failure" what she needed to know in order to reach her goal. During her husband's tenure as president, Eleanor Roosevelt campaigned for the passage of laws against racial bias; her efforts "failed," but not before laying the groundwork for the Civil Rights movement more than thirty years later.

To many, Helen Keller was doomed to a life of "failure" when, as a toddler, an illness extinguished her sight and hearing, yet she succeeded in touching millions of hearts and minds.

Victory does not require that we succeed the first time that we try, but that we persevere until the time is right. No matter how humble our endeavors, when we practice these principles, our lives become a never-ending chain of successful moments, each link necessary to the next.

I must start

by putting

one foot

in front

of the other.

SPONTANEITY

Focusing our attention—daily and

hourly—not on what is wrong,

but on what we love and value,

allows us to participate in the birth

of a better future, ushered in by the

choices we make each and every day.

—*Carol Pearson*
20th-century American business
writer and consultant

Spontaneity

Spontaneity asks us to fly in the face of the fundamental knowledge that runs our lives—the knowledge that time is passing.

We know that every minute we squander is one we'll never see again, so we try to wrench as much from our days as we can: work, kids, day care, family obligations, doctors, dentists, and, when we can squeeze it in, sleep.

Deep down, we suspect that each day is a gift, but when we're measuring time with a stopwatch, it's difficult for that knowledge to register in a conscious way. So we fantasize about island vacations and long weekends, where we're relaxed enough to feel the beauty of being alive. Getaways are good for that, of course; they lift us out of the everyday so that we see our world more clearly. Without the distraction of ringing phones, a yammering boss, or household chores, we're aware of simply being alive. Instead of schedules, we let spontaneity govern our actions. Our blood pressure evens out, our breathing deepens; the moments are golden.

We needn't wait for a planned, perfectly orchestrated moment, though, to feel this sense of peace. We can seize the moment right now. How? By allowing ourselves to be spontaneous; by not editing our joyous impulses to connect with ourselves and others, but by heeding them as if they were flares lighting the road to happiness. Unlike impulsiveness—which is often governed by whim and exerted without regard for others—spontaneity is

good-humored, asking only a pliant
nature in return for sudden, lasting
moments of joy. We heed its call when
we think of a long-gone high-school
chum and use the impetus to track her
down—right *now*; when we're rushing
to put away the groceries but pause to
savor the scent of a fresh grapefruit or
orange; when we turn off the car's air
conditioning, roll down the window,

and take a second to feel the raw, hot power of the mid-summer sun.

When, in a word, we pay attention. Simply by being on the lookout for joy, we will have more joy in our lives. We need only be open to it.

I am flexible.

We discovered in each other and ourselves

worlds, galaxies, a universe.

—*Anne Rivers Siddons (b. 1936)*
American writer

Love

To lose ourselves in another's eyes, to spend an entire afternoon dreaming about the one we love, to feel giddy with desire—such is the stuff love is made of. At work, we're absent-minded; at night, too keyed up to sleep. We look forward to the time spent together, and look back on the wonderful memories we already have.

This is the easy part of love, when it's new and effortless, pulled forward by a momentum so strong that we have no choice but to surrender to it—not that we'd want to fight the tide of feeling that registers so viscerally. We finally understand what the poets have been writing about all these years. "If this is love," we shout to the heavens, "give me more!"

Over time, however, we learn just what "more" requires from both of us. Acceptance, patience, vulnerability, kindness—especially on the days when we're so at odds with each other that we've nearly forgotten what it was that brought us together. Or when the stress of our lives leaves only enough energy to care for ourselves, not each other. During such times, we grasp

and take comfort from the real truth
about love: It is comprised of different
elements, each steering the relationship as we navigate the bracing seas
of intimacy. Commitment allows us
to feel safe as we let emotions wash
over us. Passion keeps our commitment from settling into mere duty,
and love of our individual selves
reminds us that what we bring to the

relationship is the most cherished gift
that we can give.

There may be moments when
one of the elements overwhelms the
others, and it is then that we can
work to rekindle our love through a
tender touch, a whispered word, or a
secret love note. The smallest gestures
are the most potent.

In the best of times, the different

pieces all fit together, and we feel the wonderful completeness of being in love—and loved.

I am the soul of passion.

TRUTH

[We have] no nobler function than

to defend the truth.

—Ruth McKenney (1911–1972)
American writer

Truth

We know a lie when we hear one.

"Get real," we sigh when we see product advertisements promising the impossible—creams that will make our skin look years younger, slick sports cars that will make us more attractive to the opposite sex, scrumptious snack cakes that contain a "world of fun."

"Don't lie to me," we shout when we hear politicians' pie-in-the-sky campaign promises that we know will evaporate after the election. Or when our boss tells us there's no money for a raise this year when we know better.

We live in a society where untruths are so common that we can feel trapped in a grown-up version of *The Emperor's New Clothes*, where only a child is willing to tell the truth. And yet we ourselves are not always blameless. How many casual lies do we tell in the course of a week? We say we're fine when in fact we're having a horrible day. We screen our calls to avoid unwanted conversations. We knowingly embellish gossip to make the story juicier. We argue that these "white lies" are harmless, but when we're dishonest, we set ourselves up to doubt our perceptions of what is real. The genuine looks suspect; the false, sincere. The world is confusing enough without muddling our own reality.

While bending the truth every now and then sometimes makes a situation easier to handle, it usually has the opposite effect in the long run. Over time, even "white lies" add up, not only diminishing our self-respect, but causing us to suspect others' motives as well. The ultimate cost? Our very footing in the world.

When we embrace what is real, we shine with a light that attracts seekers similar to us. Together, we acknowledge the unshakable truth: If we can't get what we want in an honest way, it is because we are not meant to have it.

We needn't dishonor ourselves with desperate wheedling or manipulation. We are cared for already. And the odds are that we will probably get much of what we want in life—and even more of what we need.

My eyes are open.

*This book has been bound using
handcraft methods, and Smyth-sewn
to ensure durability.*

*The dust jacket and interior were designed
by Nancy Loggins Gonzalez.*

*The text was written by Ronnie Polaneczky
and edited by Virginia Mattingly.*

The text was set in Galliard and Gill Sans.